This book belongs to:

_____

My First Book of
Bible Stories

written by Lori C. Froeb

illustrated by Marta Álvarez Miguéns

studio
INTERNATIONAL

Studio Fun International
An imprint of Printers Row Publishing Group
A division of Readerlink Distribution Services, LLC
9717 Pacific Heights Blvd, San Diego, CA 92121
www.studiofun.com

Printers Row Publishing Group is a division of Readerlink Distribution Services, LLC.
Studio Fun International is a registered trademark of Readerlink Distribution Services, LLC.
All notations of errors or omissions should be addressed to Studio Fun International,
Editorial Department, at the above address.
ISBN: 978-0-7944-4872-1
Manufactured, printed, and assembled in Heshan, China.
First printing, May 2022, LP/5/22
26 25 24 23 22   1 2 3 4 5

Table of Contents

Old Testament

Creation 2

Noah and the Ark 8

The Story of Abraham 13

Joseph the Dreamer 17

Moses, God's Faithful Servant 22

Balaam's Donkey 29

David and Goliath 32

Daniel in the Lions' Den 36

Jonah and the Big Fish 38

New Testament

The First Christmas 42

Fishers of Men 49

Feeding the 5,000 52

Jesus Walks on the Water 54

The Parable of the Sower 58

Jesus Rides to Jerusalem 62

The Last Supper 64

Jesus' Trial 66

The First Easter 69

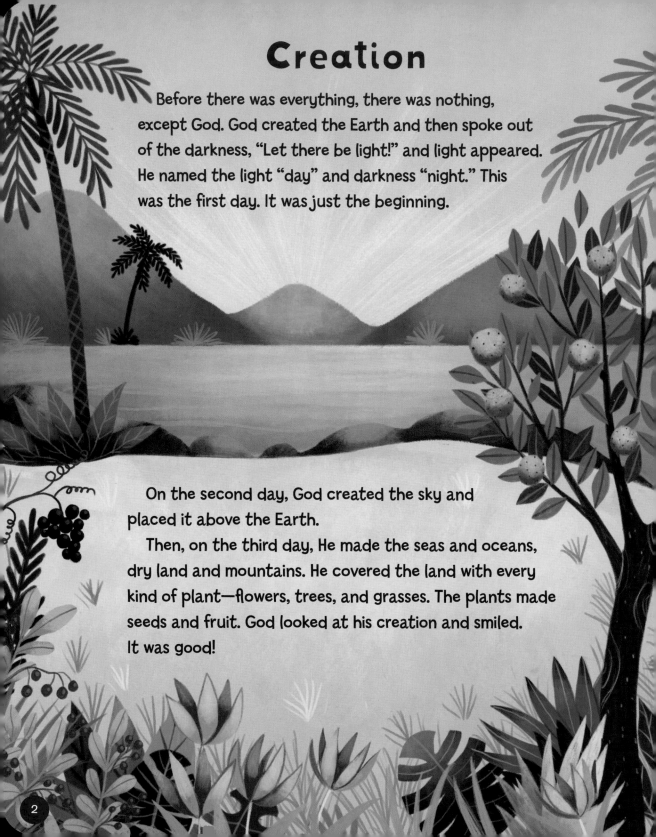

Creation

Before there was everything, there was nothing, except God. God created the Earth and then spoke out of the darkness, "Let there be light!" and light appeared. He named the light "day" and darkness "night." This was the first day. It was just the beginning.

On the second day, God created the sky and placed it above the Earth.

Then, on the third day, He made the seas and oceans, dry land and mountains. He covered the land with every kind of plant—flowers, trees, and grasses. The plants made seeds and fruit. God looked at his creation and smiled. It was good!

On the fourth day, God created the sun, moon and stars. He placed them in the sky to shine light on Earth—the sun during the day and moon and stars at night.

On the fifth day, God filled the oceans with life—fishes, whales, crabs, and sharks. "Let there be birds in the sky," He said, and birds of every kind appeared.

On the sixth day, God said, "Let the land be full of animals."
Every animal that crawls, runs, or hops appeared on the Earth. But God
wasn't finished yet. "Let us create man to watch over creation," God
said, and He formed Adam from the dust. Adam was the first man. God
gave him the job of naming all the animals and watching over them.

God saw that Adam was lonely. "I will give him a partner," God said. He made Adam fall into a deep sleep. Then God took one of Adam's ribs and created a woman from it. She was Eve, the first woman. God placed Adam and Eve in the beautiful Garden of Eden and told them to enjoy all the fruit and plants in it.

There was one rule. They were not allowed to eat from the tree of the knowledge of good and evil. If they did that, they would die.

One day, a serpent called to Eve from the forbidden tree. "God doesn't want you to eat this fruit because then you will be wise like Him," the serpent said. "Surely, you won't die."

Eve looked at the delicious fruit and couldn't resist. She took a bite and shared it with Adam. God was very angry. He made Adam and Eve leave the garden for disobeying Him. From that day on, people would no longer live forever and would have to work hard to grow food.

God made the sun,
And God made the trees.
God made the mountains,
And God made me.
Thank you, O God,
For the sun and the trees,
For making the mountains,
And for making me.
Amen

Noah and the Ark

Adam and Eve had children. Their children had children. Soon the world was full of people. But they turned away from God. One man, named Noah, still loved God. The Lord spoke to Noah one day.

"People have become evil. I am sending a flood to destroy the Earth," He said. "I want you to build a giant boat. I will keep your family and two of every animal safe on that boat." Noah was confused, but he did as God had asked. With the help of his three sons, Noah built an ark out of cypress wood and packed it with food for everyone.

When the ark was finished, God sent animals from all over the Earth to Noah. Pairs of male and female animals went into the ark. They slithered, flew, crawled, walked, and scurried into the giant boat.

When they were all safe inside, God shut the door. Soon after, rain began to fall. For 40 days, a storm raged outside the ark. The water covered the tallest mountains and trees. Nothing living was left on Earth.

God kept His promise to Noah. His family was safe. After the rains stopped, Noah sent out a dove to see if she could find dry land. Finding none, she returned. Noah tried again a week later, and the dove came back with an olive leaf in her beak. "The water is drying up!" Noah said to his wife. Seven days later, he sent the dove out again. She didn't return. Soon after, the ark came to rest on the top of Mount Ararat.

When the ground was dry, Noah, his family, and all the animals walked out of the boat onto dry land. Noah built an altar to the Lord and praised Him for His goodness. God saw the altar and was pleased. He made a promise to Noah, "I will never flood the Earth again."

Then He put a beautiful rainbow in the sky and said, "Whenever a rainbow appears in the sky, I will remember this promise I have made."

Thank you for the
world so sweet.
Thank you for the food
we eat.
Thank you for the
birds that sing.
Thank you, God, for
everything.
Amen

E. Rutter Leatham

The Story of Abraham

Many years later, God chose a man named Abraham to be the father of His people. Abraham and his wife Sarah had no children. They were both very old.

"You will have a son," the Lord said to him. "And you will name him Isaac."

"How can this be?" Abraham asked God.

Sarah laughed when she heard the news. She was 90 years old, and Abraham was 100!

13

Just as the Lord had promised, Sarah had a baby boy. Abraham named him Isaac as God commanded. Abraham loved his son very, very much. When Isaac was a boy, God tested Abraham.

"Bring your son to a place I will show you," the Lord said. "Build an altar and offer Isaac as a sacrifice."

Abraham could not believe what he was hearing, but he packed what he needed and set out with the boy.

Abraham built an altar in the place God showed him. He placed wood on it, then laid his son gently on top. He raised his knife. Then God called out, "Abraham! Don't hurt the boy."

Abraham stopped and saw a ram caught in some thorns. He sacrificed it instead.

"You have proven how much you love me," God said. "I will bless you and all your descendants because you obeyed."

Now I lay me
Down to sleep.
I pray the Lord
My soul to keep.
Your love be with me
Through the night,
And wake me with
The morning light.
Amen

Joseph the Dreamer

A man named Israel had 12 sons. His favorite was named Joseph. Israel made Joseph a colorful coat and gave it to him as a gift. When Joseph's brothers saw the beautiful coat, they were jealous and angry. They hated their brother.

Joseph often had dreams. He told his brothers that he dreamed they were harvesting grain together. His bundle of grain stood up and all his brothers' bundles bowed down to it.

"Do you plan to rule over us?" his brothers asked. This made them hate Joseph even more.

The brothers planned to get rid of Joseph. When Joseph came looking for his brothers in the field, they grabbed him. They tore off his coat, threw him in a well, and left him there to die.

But when they saw a group of travelers passing through the area, they changed their minds. They sold Joseph to them. Then the brothers tore up the beautiful coat and rubbed animal blood on it. They went home and showed their father the bloody coat. Israel believed his beloved son was dead.

The travelers brought Joseph to Egypt and sold him to Potiphar, one of Pharaoh's guards. God never left Joseph and helped him be successful in everything he did for Potiphar. Joseph was no longer a slave. Potiphar put him in charge of his house and fields.

One day, Potiphar's wife told a lie about Joseph. Potiphar believed her and put him in jail. Even in jail, God was with Joseph. The warden trusted Joseph and put him in charge of the other prisoners. One day, Pharaoh had a dream that he couldn't figure out. He sent for Joseph.

"I heard you can figure out what dreams mean," said Pharaoh.

"I can't on my own, but with God's help I can," answered Joseph.

Pharaoh told Joseph his dream about seven skinny cows eating seven fat cows. Joseph told him that the dream meant there would be seven years of famine after seven good years. If Pharaoh didn't prepare, Egypt would not have enough food to eat.

Pharaoh was impressed and put Joseph in charge of Egypt. Only Pharaoh was more powerful. Joseph prepared Egypt for the famine. In seven years, it came just as the dream had said.

Joseph's family was starving. They traveled to Egypt to buy food. As they bowed in front of Joseph to ask for grain, the brothers didn't realize he was their brother. But Joseph recognized them.

"It's me!" Joseph said, "I'm the brother you sold so long ago. God has blessed me. You sold me as a slave, but now I'm a ruler of Egypt!"

Joseph forgave his brothers and hugged them. He made sure his family had a home and everything they could want in Egypt. God took Joseph's bad situation and turned it into something good.

Moses, God's Faithful Servant

Over many years, the children of Israel, called Hebrews, filled Egypt. Pharaoh saw how many there were and he was afraid they would rise up against him. He forced the Hebrews to be slaves and ordered that all baby boys be thrown into the river.

One Hebrew woman had a baby boy. To save his life, she tucked him into a basket and placed him in the river. His sister Miriam hid in the reeds and watched to see what would happen to him.

Pharaoh's daughter was bathing in the river that day. She spotted the basket in the reeds and heard the baby crying inside. When she opened it, she saw him.

"He's a Hebrew baby," she said to her servants.

Miriam came out of the reeds and asked the princess if she'd like a Hebrew woman to nurse the baby. The princess agreed and gave the baby to his mother. When he was older, the boy became the princess's son. She named the boy Moses, which means "I took him from the water."

Moses grew up in the palace, but he knew that he was Hebrew. When he saw an Egyptian beating a Hebrew slave, he became angry. He killed the Egyptian, then ran away from Egypt.

Moses became a shepherd. One day, Moses saw a bush that was on fire. He was curious. The bush wasn't burning. When he got close, God spoke to him from the bush, saying, "I want you to bring my people out of Egypt."

Moses was not sure why God had chosen him, but God promised to be with him. He would help Moses convince Pharaoh to let the Israelites go.

Pharaoh didn't want to hear what Moses had to say. "I will not let your people go!" he said. Then he made the slaves work even harder.

God heard the cry of His people. He sent ten terrible plagues on Egypt. The river turned to blood, frogs covered the land, people got painful sores, and hail fell from the sky. Pharaoh still would not let the Hebrews go. When God caused all of Egypt's firstborn sons to die, Pharaoh finally said, "Leave this place and take all the Israelites with you!"

The Israelites left Egypt. It wasn't long before Pharaoh changed his mind. His chariots raced after them. When the Israelites got to the Red Sea, they were trapped between Pharaoh's army and the water. God told Moses to stretch his staff over the sea. When he did this, a great wind blew and parted the water. The people walked across the sea on dry land.

The Israelites were safe. When Pharaoh's army charged after them, the strong wind blew again and the walls of water rushed back into the sea. Every Egyptian drowned, and the Israelites sang a song of praise to the Lord.

The Israelites had been traveling for months when they came to Mount Sinai. The top of the mountain was covered with smoke. Lightning flashed and thunder boomed from it because God had come down to the mountain.

God called Moses to climb to the top. Moses was on the mountain for 40 days and nights. While he was there, God gave Moses His rules for the Israelites. The Lord Himself wrote 10 of these rules on two stone tablets. They were the Ten Commandments. When Moses brought them to the people, his face was shining with God's glory.

The Ten Commandments

I am the Lord your God.
There are no other gods before me.

Do not make statues to worship.

Do not misuse God's name.

Keep the seventh day, the Sabbath,
as a day of rest.

Respect your mother and father.

Do not kill.

Do not want someone else's husband or wife.

Do not steal.

Do not say false things about your neighbor.

Do not desire your neighbor's things.

Balaam's Donkey

The Israelites set up camp in Moab. King Balak of Moab was troubled. He was afraid the Israelites would become too powerful. He sent messengers to Balaam, a man who was able to bless and curse people. The king wanted Balaam to curse the Israelites in return for gold and riches. Balaam answered that he could only do what the Lord commanded him.

God's message to Balaam was clear, "Do not curse my people. I have blessed them."

When Balaam refused the king's offer, Balak offered Balaam even more riches. Again, God told Balaam not to curse the people, but to follow the king's messengers to Moab.

Balaam was riding his donkey on the road to Moab, when she suddenly stopped. An angel with a sword stood in her way. Balaam didn't see the angel. He beat the donkey to make her keep walking. Twice more the donkey stopped, and twice more Balaam hit her. Then something amazing happened.

The donkey opened her mouth to speak! "What have I done to make you hit me three times?" she said. "You have ridden me many times before. Have I ever stopped like this?"

"No," was Balaam's answer.

God opened Balaam's eyes, and he saw the angel in front of him. "Why did you beat your donkey?" the angel asked. "I came to stop you from cursing God's people. If your donkey hadn't stopped, I would have killed you."

Balaam realized he was wrong. The angel told him to go to Moab and follow the Lord's instructions.

When Balaam got to Moab, the king asked him to curse the Israelites three times. Each time, Balaam blessed them instead. When Balak asked Balaam why he wasn't doing as he was asked, Balaam answered, "I told you, I must do what the Lord commands."

David and Goliath

When Saul was the king of Israel, the Philistine army showed up for battle. They brought Goliath—a giant. He wore heavy armor and carried a giant spear. The Philistines had a challenge for Saul. He must choose one of his men to battle the giant. If Goliath won, Saul's people would become the Philistines' servants. If Saul's soldier won, the Philistines would serve Saul. The king and his people were terrified.

David was a young shepherd boy who played music for the king. When he heard about Goliath's challenge, he spoke to Saul.

"I will fight the giant," David said. When Saul told him that he was too young to fight, David answered, "I have killed lions and bears to protect my sheep. God protected me then, and He will protect me now."

Saul put David in his own armor and helmet, and gave him his sword. But David wasn't used to those things. He took them off, grabbed his staff and sling, and gathered five smooth river stones. Then he went to meet Goliath.

Goliath laughed when he saw David. "You come to fight me with sticks? Do you think I'm a dog?"

David answered, "You come against me with swords and spears, but I come against you in the name of the Lord."

Goliath huffed and prepared to attack. David took one of the stones, put it into his sling, and let it fly. The stone hit Goliath in the forehead and the great giant fell to the ground, dead. Seeing this, the rest of the Philistine army ran away. After Saul died, the shepherd boy David became the king of Israel.

23rd Psalm

The Lord is my shepherd, I lack nothing.
He makes me lie down in green pastures,
he leads me beside quiet waters,
he refreshes my soul.
He guides me along the right paths
for his name's sake.
Even though I walk
through the darkest valley,
I will fear no evil,
For you are with me;
your rod and your staff,
they comfort me.
You prepare a table before me
in the presence of my enemies.
You anoint my head with oil;
my cup overflows.
Surely your goodness and love will follow me
all the days of my life,
and I will dwell in the house of the **LORD** forever.

Psalm 23 (NIV)

Daniel in the Lions' Den

Daniel was an important man to King Darius. The king trusted him and planned to put Daniel in charge of the whole kingdom. This made the king's other men jealous. They knew Daniel was a man of God. They convinced the king to make a new rule: anyone who worshiped anyone but King Darius would be thrown into the lions' den.

Daniel did not stop praying to God. When the men told King Darius this, the king had no choice. He could not go back on his law. Sadly, he sent Daniel to the lion's den, saying, "May your God rescue you!"

King Darius could not sleep. In the morning, he hurried to the den. He couldn't believe what he saw. Daniel was calmly sitting with the lions!

"I am all right!" Daniel said. "God sent an angel to close the lions' mouths."

The king ordered the evil men to be thrown into the lions' den. Then he made a new law for his people: "Everyone must worship Daniel's God. He is the true God who saved Daniel from the lions."

Jonah and the Big Fish

God had a job for a man named Jonah, "Go to the wicked city of Nineveh and preach my word."

Jonah didn't want to go to Nineveh. He decided to run from God. Jonah got on a boat that was sailing far away from the sinful city. While he was on the boat, God sent a giant storm. The wind and waves tossed the boat so much the sailors were afraid it would sink. They threw everything they could find overboard.

Jonah was asleep below the deck. When the men woke him up, Jonah told them that the storm was his fault. He knew God was angry because he had disobeyed Him.

"Throw me into the sea," Jonah said, "and the storm will stop." The men did as Jonah asked, and the water became still. As Jonah sank, God sent a giant fish to save him. The fish swallowed Jonah and disappeared into the sea.

Jonah was inside the fish's belly for three days and nights. Jonah knew he had been wrong. He prayed to the Lord from inside the fish, "When I was in trouble, you saved me. I will praise you and do as you ask."

God saw that Jonah had learned his lesson. He told the fish to spit out Jonah on the sand. Then He told Jonah again to go to Nineveh to tell the people to turn from their evil ways or the city would be destroyed. This time, Jonah did what God commanded him, and Nineveh was saved.

Trust in the Lord
with all your heart
And lean not on
your own understanding;
In all your ways
submit to him,
And he will make your
paths straight.

Proverbs 3:5-7 (NIV)

The First Christmas

A young woman named Mary was at her house when someone special came to visit. He was an angel named Gabriel sent by God. Mary was afraid. She had never seen an angel before.

"Don't be afraid," Gabriel said. "God has chosen you to be the mother of a special baby boy. He will be God's Son, Jesus!"

Mary didn't understand, but she trusted God. "I am the Lord's servant," she answered. "May what you say come true."

Mary was engaged to a man named Joseph. Before Mary's baby was born, the Roman emperor Caesar demanded that everyone go to their hometowns to be counted. Joseph was from Bethlehem, so he and Mary needed to travel there. They packed their things and started their long journey.

It took them many days to get to Bethlehem. When they arrived, all the inns were full of people that were in town to be counted. Mary and Joseph had no place to stay.

No Room

It was almost time for the baby to born, and Mary needed to rest. They found a stable where horses and other animals were kept. It was warm and dry, and the hay made a soft bed on the ground.

Mary had her baby while they were in Bethlehem. She wrapped Him snuggly in cloth and laid Him in the manger. She named Him Jesus, just as the angel had told her to do.

Shepherds were watching their sheep in the fields not far away.
Suddenly, an angel appeared. The shepherds were frightened.

The angel spoke in a loud voice, "I bring you great news! A Savior has
been born tonight! You will find Him in a manger, wrapped in cloths."

The shepherds watched in wonder as angels filled the sky.
They were singing, "Glory to God in the highest!"

When the angels were gone, the shepherds talked among themselves. "Let's go see the baby the angel told us about!"

When they got to the stable, they found Jesus with His mother and Joseph. They knew He was the baby the angel talked about because He was sleeping in the manger.

When the shepherds left, they told anyone they could find about the baby. Everyone who heard their story was amazed. The shepherds returned to their sheep and praised God for sending a Savior to men.

Wise men from the East called magi had noticed a new bright star in the sky. They knew it meant a king had been born. They wanted to see the new king for themselves, so they followed the star. They traveled until the star stopped above a house. There they found Jesus and His mother.

The magi were filled with happiness. They bowed down in front of Jesus and worshiped Him. Then they gave Him the gifts they brought—gold, frankincense, and myrrh. They left the house with joy in their hearts.

Be near me, Lord Jesus,
I ask Thee to stay
Close by me forever,
and love me, I pray.
Bless all the dear children
in Thy tender care,
And fit us for heaven
to live with Thee there.
Amen.

Fishers of Men

One morning, Jesus was preaching to a crowd of people next to a lake. There were fishermen nearby. Jesus got into one of their boats and asked a fisherman named Simon to take Him away from shore. Then Jesus spoke to the people from the boat.

When He was finished, Jesus spoke to Simon and the other fishermen, "Bring the boat to deep water and put your nets down to catch some fish."

Simon answered Jesus, "We spent all night fishing and didn't even catch one fish. But we will do as you ask."

The fishermen sailed to the deepest part of the lake, and threw the nets into the water. It didn't take long for the nets to fill with fish. There were so many, the nets began to break.

Simon asked a boat nearby to help Him. When they were all done pulling up the nets, the boats were so full of fish that they both began to sink!

Simon and his fellow fishermen, James and John, were amazed at all the fish. Simon fell to his knees in front of Jesus and said, "Lord, leave me. I am sinful."

Jesus looked at Simon and answered, "Simon, do not fear. From this day on you will be a fisher of men!" Then He told Simon, James, and John to follow Him. They left their boats and everything they had to follow Jesus. They were His first disciples.

Feeding the 5,000

Jesus almost always had lots of people around Him. One afternoon, He was with a giant crowd of 5,000 people, healing the sick. The sun was starting to go down.

"Jesus," said one of his disciples, "it's late and we don't have any food to feed all these people. Send them to the villages so they can buy food."

"Don't send them away," Jesus said. "You give them food."

The disciples were confused, "We only have five loaves of bread and two fish. There are thousands of people!"

Jesus asked them to bring the bread and fish to Him. He said a prayer and began breaking the loaves and fish into pieces. Then He told His disciples to bring some food to every person in the crowd.

Everyone ate until they were full. When they were finished, there were 12 baskets of food left over. It was a miracle!

Jesus Walks on the Water

After Jesus fed the 5,000, He told his disciples to get into a boat and start sailing across the lake. Then He went to a mountain to pray. When He was finished, it was dark. The boat was far away from shore. A strong wind was blowing, and the water was full of waves.

Just before the sun rose, Jesus stepped into the lake to meet His friends. Instead of sinking, Jesus' feet stayed on the surface of the water as He walked to the boat.

When the disciples saw Jesus walking on the water, they were frightened. "It must be a ghost!" they cried.

"Don't be afraid!" Jesus called to them. "It's me!"

Peter wasn't so sure. "Lord, if it is really you, tell me to come to you."

Jesus told him to come. Peter took a deep breath and carefully got out of the boat.

He didn't sink! He walked on the water toward Jesus. But when he noticed the wind swirling around him and waves splashing on his feet, he was afraid. Then Peter began to sink.

"Save me, Lord!" Peter cried.

Jesus grabbed Peter's hand and pulled him up. "Why did you not believe?" He asked Peter.

When they got back into the boat, the wind stopped and the water was still. The disciples worshiped Jesus after what they had seen.

The Lord's Prayer

Our Father in heaven,

hallowed be your name,

your kingdom come,

your will be done,

on earth as it is in heaven.

Give us today our daily bread.

And forgive us our debts,

as we also have

forgiven our debtors.

And lead us not into temptation,

but deliver us from the evil one.

Amen

Matthew 6:9–13 (NIV)

The Parable of the Sower

Jesus often told stories called parables to help people understand God's Word. One day, He was teaching a crowd. He told them to listen closely as He told a parable about a farmer sowing seeds.

The farmer went out to his field with a big bag of seeds and scattered them as he walked. Some of the seeds fell on the walking path. The ground was hard and the seeds' roots could not push into the soil. Birds came and ate up the seeds before they had a chance to grow.

Some of the seeds fell on rocky soil. They started to grow, but the rocks were in the way of their roots and they couldn't find water. They soon died in the hot sun.

Other seeds fell among thorny plants. The seeds were able to grow, but they didn't get enough light to grow grain.

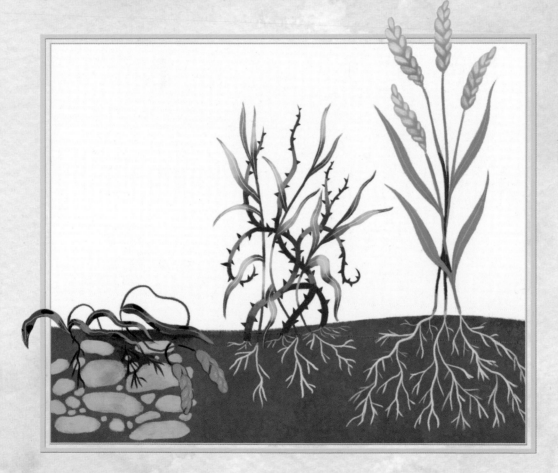

Finally, some of the seeds landed on soft soil. The seeds' roots dug deep to find water. The plants grew big and strong. When it was harvest time, those plants gave the farmer back thirty, sixty, and a hundred times more grain than he sowed.

When Jesus was finished, He said, "Whoever has ears to hear, let them hear." The disciples were confused by the story, so Jesus explained it. He said that the seeds that fell on the path are like the people who hear God's word and don't understand it. The seeds that landed in the rocky soil are like the people who hear God's word and are excited about it. But when those people start having problems in their lives, they forget God's word.

The seeds that were scattered into the thorns are like the people who hear God's word and understand it. But instead of sharing God's word with others, those people let money or other things have all their attention.

The seeds that fell on the good soil are like the people who hear God's word and are so excited about it, they never stop learning. They can't wait to tell others about God and help make His kingdom grow.

Jesus Rides to Jerusalem

Jesus and His disciples were on their way to Jerusalem when Jesus said to them, "There is a donkey in the town nearby. Bring it to me."

The disciples found the donkey tied in its pen. When the owner asked them why they were taking his donkey, they said, "The Lord needs it."

They brought the donkey to Jesus and covered its back with their cloaks for Jesus to sit on.

As Jesus rode the donkey on the road to Jerusalem, people spread their cloaks on the ground and waved palm branches in the air. They praised Jesus, saying, "Hosanna! Blessed is the King!"

There were religious leaders called Pharisees in the crowd. They did not like Jesus' message. They demanded that Jesus make the people stop.

Jesus answered them, saying, "If they were quiet, the rocks would call out instead."

The Last Supper

Jesus and His disciples were having Passover dinner together when Jesus picked up a piece of bread. He blessed it, then passed it around, saying, "This is my body that is given for you." Then Jesus held a cup filled with wine. "This is my blood that is given to save many," He said, then passed it around.

Jesus told His disciples that whenever they eat bread and drink wine like this, they should remember Him. He also told them that one of them would turn against Him before the next morning.

After dinner, they all went to a place called Gethsemane. Jesus told his disciples to wait while He prayed. While Jesus was praying, a crowd with swords and clubs came. Judas, one of Jesus' disciples, was with them. Judas said to the priests in the crowd, "I will kiss the man you should arrest." Then He walked up to Jesus and kissed Him. Jesus was arrested and taken away.

Jesus' Trial

Jesus was brought to a high priest named Caiaphas. He had been trying to get rid of Jesus for a long time. When Jesus called Himself the Son of God, Caiaphas charged Him with blasphemy, which is speaking against God. Then he sent Jesus to Pilate, the Roman governor, to be put to death.

Pilate wasn't sure what to do. Jesus hadn't committed any crime. There was a crowd gathered for a festival in the city. Pilate brought out Jesus and another famous criminal named Barabbas. He asked the crowd who they wanted set free. "Barabbas!" they shouted.

"What should I do with Jesus?" Pilate asked them.

"Crucify him!" was their answer.

Pilate had no choice but to send Jesus to death. The soldiers whipped Jesus and put a crown of thorns on His head. Then they made Him carry a heavy cross through the city and up a hill called Golgatha. There, they nailed him to the cross. "Forgive them," Jesus prayed to His Father. "They don't know what they are doing."

As Jesus hung on the cross, the sky grew dark even though it was still the afternoon. "It is finished!" Jesus said, then died. An earthquake shook the ground and the people were terrified. "He truly was God's Son!" said one of the guards.

A kind man named Joseph took Jesus' body and wrapped it in cloth. He put Jesus in a tomb carved into the rock and rolled a giant stone in front of the entrance. Pilate put guards at the tomb so no one could take Jesus' body.

The First Easter

Three days later, Mary went to the tomb with Mary Magdalene. When they got there, the stone was rolled away. An angel stood at the tomb.

"He isn't here," the angel said. "He has risen! Go and tell the others."

Mary and Mary Magdalene were overjoyed! They ran to tell the disciples what they had seen. Later, Jesus appeared to them all and told them to spread His message of God's love to everyone. "I will always be with you," He said, "even to the end of time."

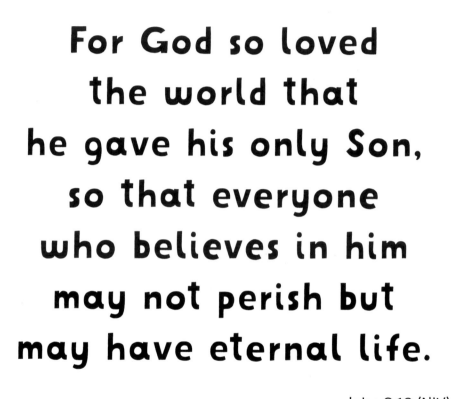

For God so loved
the world that
he gave his only Son,
so that everyone
who believes in him
may not perish but
may have eternal life.

John 3:16 (NIV)